who KNEW

Extreme
Coupons

A Step-by-Step
Guide to Saving
Thousands on
Groceries

Bruce Lubin & Jeanne Bossolina-Lubin

CASTLE POINT PUBLISHING

TABLE OF CONTENTS

Introduction

If you've ever felt a tiny thrill when you hand over a coupon to the cashier and watch your total go down, you're going to love this book. If you've been looking for a relatively easy way to drastically cut your budget, you're going to love it even more! Couponing is not only fun—it can save you thousands of dollars per year at the supermarket and beyond.

We'll admit it, we were never huge couponers. But as many of you know, we love finding ways to save money, and using coupons was something we couldn't ignore—especially after watching our friends walk away with a thousand dollars' worth of groceries for less than $50. A few Sunday papers later and we were walking out of our local drugstore with eleven items that, after cash-back coupons, we didn't pay a cent for.

If you're just looking for a few easy ways to knock money off your receipt, this book will give you everything you need. For instance, did you know that when you get one of those "$2 off your next purchase" coupons, many drugstores will let you use it right there and then, as long as you make another transaction? We'll give you lots of tips like this, including where to look in your supermarket for the lowest prices, and how to find online coupons in seconds.

But if you're willing to devote a few hours each month to couponing, we can help you take your savings even further. Want to never pay full price for just about every grocery item you buy? Want to learn how to stack your coupons so that you'll have more than one for every product in your pantry? We'll show you how—and we'll also give you our best tips for organizing your coupons, creating a stockpile, and finding more coupons than you ever thought possible.

Whether you decide to go the casual route or go pro, you'll love the satisfaction you'll get from using coupons. As casual couponers, we loved being able to load coupons right onto our grocery savings card from the internet, and knowing that as long as we had our coupon wallet with us in the car, we could save some money even if we had to quickly run into the store. As extreme couponers, we love the ability to rein in our budget without having to make any sacrifices. We also love having our own stockpile to "shop" from at home when we need something. Just wait until the first time your kid gets the flu and you don't have to run to the store to get any cough syrup, and you'll know what we mean. Not to mention, you'll be the most emergency-prepared person on the block!

What couponing is really about is strategy, so the good news is that once you read this book (it will go fast, we promise), you'll be saving without barely any work at all. Not only will you be privy to some of the secrets about sales and loyalty programs that even the stores don't want you to know about, but you'll have access to everything you need online to get started. Just visit WhoKnewTips.com/ExtremeCoupons and you'll find a list of more than 180 websites where you can get free coupons directly from manufacturers, as well as 150 more that link to blogs that will tell you what's on sale at your local supermarket, and which recent coupons you can use for those very same items.

If you have any questions as you go along, we're always here to help! Visit us at Facebook.com/WhoKnewTips and let us know about your couponing journey—or just brag about the savings on your most recent grocery receipt!

Thriftily Yours,
Bruce and Jeanne

CHAPTER 1

The Art of Couponing: Easy-to-Use Coupon Strategy Tips

I t seems simple on the face of it: Hand over a coupon for a few cents off a product, then get that product at a discount. But with a few easy strategies, you can go from getting just a few cents off to getting all of your products at half off or more—and some things even for free! But before you run off to the grocery store, the first step in your journey to big savings is learning the three basic coupon strategy tips that make extreme couponing possible—stacking, stockpiling, and knowing what coupons to save.

Stacking Coupons

It's the joy of every couponer: two coupons for the same thing! Many novice coupon-clippers don't realize that it's almost always possible to use more than one coupon per item (called "stacking" coupons)—even if your coupon says "limit one." That's because most stores allow you to use a manufacturer coupon (like the kind that come in the Sunday paper) with a store coupon (like the kind that come in flyers from the store).

The reason why companies release coupons is to get you hooked on their products—so don't be surprised if they've also offered your local store an incentive to offer their own coupons or put the product on sale, too. Coupons + sales = big savings for you! Each

week, compare the coupons we'll teach you to save with flyers you've received for in-store sales for the week— or better yet, just check with one of the many coupon matchup sites we've listed at the back of this book. This easy step will immediately save you twice as much or more on every product you buy.

EXTREME TIP

It's no surprise that for the biggest savings, you should have a stack of coupons at least two deep for every product you buy. Couponers who consider themselves "pro" often wouldn't be caught dead buying something with only one coupon—unless the item is also on sale! Keep reading to find out how.

What Should I Clip?

When clipping coupons, our rule of thumb is "Clip coupons for any product you would use." Along with this, if you consider yourself someone who's only willing to buy certain brands of household products, now may be the time to break that habit. Start exploring different brands to find more than one you like, and you'll find more ways to save. Of course, we all have our favorite brand of granola bars, mac and cheese, and much more. But if you can live with several different

manufacturers of products like paper towels and plastic bags, as well as various cereals, desserts, and premade meals, you'll find many more coupons you can use.

KNOWING YOUR COUPONS' RESTRICTIONS

Once you have a ton of coupons, how do you know which ones you can stack on top of each other, allowing you to use more than one coupon for the same product? Take a look at what the coupons say to see how you can use them:

✦ **NO RESTRICTIONS.** If your coupon doesn't have any restrictions listed on it, that means you can use as many you want when purchasing a single item.

✦ **ONE PER PURCHASE.** The most common type of restriction, this means that you can only use one of these for each item you purchase. However, you can use multiple coupons if you are buying multiple items. For example, if you're buying five tubes of toothpaste and you have five identical coupons, you can use all of them.

✦ **ONE PER ORDER/ONE PER TRANSACTION.** These coupons can only be used once for each transaction you make at the register. At some stores, they will allow you

to make two or more transactions (paying for various parts of your purchase separately) to use all your coupons. At others, you'll have to leave and come back to the store some other time to use a duplicate coupon again.

✦ ONE PER HOUSEHOLD. These limited-use coupons only allow you to use them once, and often have a special ID code on them or ask you to fill in your name and address. It seem like a shame you can only use them one time and one time only, but they're usually very high value.

✦ DO NOT DOUBLE. If your grocery store doubles coupons, this restrictions means that they can't double this particular coupon.

Keep in mind, no matter what kind of coupon it is, you can almost always stack a coupon from a store flyer with a coupon from the manufacturer! And many times, you can stack a "physical" coupon with an online one.

Stockpiling

If you've seen extreme couponers on TV, you've seen their stockpiles. Famously taking up entire spare rooms, basements, and garages, these shelves of everyday items are often the pride of extreme couponers. While your stockpile doesn't have to be more than a several shelves or a few plastic storage containers, it's important to have a space where you can store items that you've bought on sale. That way, you can stock up essentials like canned goods when you find the absolute lowest price—making sure that you never have to buy them at full price again. Only buying items when they're on sale is an important part of making extreme couponing work for you, so you'll definitely need to stock up when you find those rock-bottom prices.

WHO KNEW?

Stockpiles can be all sorts of shapes and sizes. The more organized they are, the easier they'll be to use. Find more hints and tips about stockpiles in the Organizing Your Coupons and Stockpile chapter.

CHAPTER 2

Where to Find Coupons

When it comes to finding coupons, there are two major areas to cover: both regular or "physical" coupons, and online coupons, which you will usually print out. This chapter covers both types, but first we'll cover online coupons.

Online Coupons

Printing out coupons from your computer can often be even easier than finding them in your Sunday paper. Just visit one of the many coupon sites like Coupons.com, RedPlum.com, and SmartSource.com, and print out the coupons right from your printer. Some sites will even allow you to add coupons to your grocery store's rewards card. Enter the ID number on the back of your card, pick the coupons you want to "clip," and their amounts will come off your total when you're rung up. For our list of the best sites to get coupons from, visit WhoKnewTips.com/ExtremeCoupons.

EXTREME TIP

If you have a smartphone, coupon clipping just got even easier. With apps from sites like Coupons.com, you can add coupons to your store's reward card without even having to get on your computer. A great pastime while you're waiting on your kids!

WHO KNEW?

Fake coupons abound on the internet, so make sure yours are the real deal. If they are a very high value or don't expire for a year or more, be suspicious. We've tested all the sites in this book, so you know they're safe!

PRINTING ONLINE COUPONS

Getting your printer to actually work correctly is hard enough, but unfortunately it's a little harder than that to make sure you can print out coupons from websites. Because companies want to make sure their coupons aren't misused, there are specific ways you have to print out most coupons that you'll find online. Most involve downloading coupon-printing software onto your computer. (You should always be careful when downloading software onto your computer, but we've tested all the sites mentioned in this book, so you can be sure they're safe.) If you're having trouble getting the software to work on your computer, check out the site's Help section. Many times, shutting down your computer and restarting it will fix the problem. Unfortunately, if you don't have a high-speed internet connection, it may be very hard for you to print coupons from the internet.

WHO KNEW?

It's perfectly fine to print out coupons in black and white ink only (and it will save you money on printer cartridges!). But you should never try to photocopy a coupon you've printed out online. Companies use a technology that will allow the store's scanner to know if a coupon has been photocopied, and it won't work.

ONLINE COUPON SECRETS

Now that we've covered the not-so-fun part about printing out coupons, here's the fun stuff: You can print out just about all internet coupons two times from each computer. Just click your internet browser's "Back" button, or go back to the site's homepage and search for the coupon again.

If you have more than one computer in your home, you can print two more coupons from that computer! Also make sure to take advantage of printers at places you are regularly, like a parent's house or college computer lab. If it's OK with your boss, you can even print out two more coupons at work!

When you're digging for online coupons, there's one last tip you should be aware of. You'll notice that when you log on to most coupon sites, they'll ask you to enter your zip code before showing you a selection

of coupons. But here's a secret they don't want you to know: While the coupon company only wants certain zip codes to access certain coupons, your grocery store doesn't know the difference! When printing out coupons from sites like Coupons.com and RedPlum.com, try typing in a few different zip codes to see what coupons crop up. If it won't let you enter a new zip code, try logging out and logging back in, or clearing the "cookies" out of your internet browser's history. Some extreme couponers will even have a few different email addresses so they can have several log-in names for different zip codes.

EXTREME TIP

Some websites, like TheCouponClippers.com, allow you to buy coupons! It may sound crazy, but if you find a really good coupon offer (or the coupon clippers have found one for you), it can be worth it to spend a few cents per coupon to get more. Prices vary by how rare the coupon is, and some sites may also charge a small "admin" fee for each order. (Because it's against companies' rules to sell coupons, you're really just paying for the service's time to clip them.) We recently spent around $3 to get more than $24 in coupons for products we buy regularly! For more sites that sell coupons, just visit us at WhoKnewTips.com/ExtremeCoupons.

WHO KNEW?

When you find an online coupon you know you're going to want to use, try to print it out as soon as possible. Most online coupons only allow a certain number of print-outs, and once they're gone, they're gone!

Physical Coupons

Even with the ease of online coupons, physical coupons—the old-fashioned kind that are already printed out, of course—are still a huge source of discounts and an essential part of any couponer's repertoire. If you're interested in getting into couponing big-time, the insert from your paper's Sunday edition is a must. Many papers offer Sunday- or weekend-only subscriptions that will pay for their own cost after using the coupons you'll find inside.

Some weekends, you'll find that your Sunday paper has so many coupon inserts that it's worth it to get more than one paper! Plan ahead by visiting a website that will tell you what coupons are going to be offered in your upcoming Sunday paper. One of our favorites is SundayCouponPreview.com. Sunday Coupon Preview has yearly schedule of coupon inserts from companies like Proctor & Gamble and General Mills, and coupon

distribution companies SmartSource and RedPlum. The site will also tell you what coupons are going to be offered in the current week's paper.

WHO KNEW?

More coupons are released in the Sunday paper in January than in any other month. More coupons are also available at the beginning of each month, so make sure to get a Sunday paper during these times for the most savings!

STORE COUPONS

Our favorite kind of coupons are store-specific coupons that are usually found in that particular store's weekly circular or on their website. That's because these coupons can almost always be used alongside manufacturer coupons (unless otherwise stated on or near the coupon).

If you don't receive the store's circular at your home, visit the store's website to find your local circular as well as any exclusive online coupons. As you go through your store's circulars to look for coupons, you'll want to check out their weekly sale items as well. (See Chapter 5: The Secrets About Sales and Loyalty Programs for everything you need to know about sales cycles and

coupon matchups.) As you become a more experienced couponer, you'll find that syncing up the coupons you have with sales that are being offered by your store is key for experiencing the biggest savings.

BEYOND THE SUNDAY PAPER

Does your supermarket have devices in the aisles that dispense coupons? Called "blinkies" by couponers because they usually have blinking lights on top of them, these machines are a great source of physical coupons. Make sure to check them out while you're on your shopping trip, and don't be afraid to take two (or three, or four!). Most don't expire for several weeks or even a month, so save them for a future trip and see if you can find a coupon online or in a coupon insert to stack on top of it!

Another place to find coupons while you're shopping is on the products themselves. These peel-off coupons are usually on the front of a product and are brightly colored, so make sure to keep an eye out for them. Be warned: It's not considered very polite to take coupons for products you aren't buying! Unlike with blinkies, "peelies" aren't meant to be taken and shared. Most of the time, you'll just want to use them when you get up to the check-out line rather than saving them for later.

Finding tear-pad coupons is a bit like winning the lottery for a couponer. These pads of coupons you can tear off are rare, but you'll sometimes find them on the edges of shelves in the supermarket. Make sure to keep an look-out for these price-busters, and take as many as you want!

WHO KNEW?

When at the store, it's not a bad idea to stop by the customer service desk and ask about coupons. Occasionally, they may have additional rebate forms for various products that they have in the store. Pamphlets that are found near the pharmacy counter may also contain coupons for over-the-counter medications and medical supplies.

WHO KNEW?

We love *All You* magazine for its thrifty tips, but did you know that is also contains anywhere from $40–$100 worth of coupons each month? At less than $2 per issue if you subscribe, this favorite of couponers is definitely worth checking out.

EASY WAYS TO SUPERCHARGE YOUR COUPON STOCKPILE

What if you're clipping coupons from your Sunday paper, checking your store's circular, and printing coupons from the internet, but you still don't feel like you have enough to make a dent?

First of all, make sure your coworkers, friends, relatives, and neighbors all know that you're a coupon-clipper, and ask them to save any coupon inserts they have. Perhaps it's their guilt at not taking advantage of coupons themselves, but you'll be surprised how many extra coupons you'll receive from others! Here are a few other suggestions for getting as many coupons as possible. The bigger your coupon stash, the better chance you'll have of doubling up coupons and saving big!

✦ **TRADE WITH YOUR FRIENDS.** In one of our favorite movies, *Mr. Mom*, Michael Keaton starts a poker game where coupons are used instead of money. While you don't necessarily have to gamble for them, trading coupons with friends is a great way to get rid of coupons you don't need and get some you do in return. If you don't have many friends who coupon, consider starting a group and teaching them what you've learned

about coupons to get them started! MeetUp.org is a great place to find and organize groups in your neighborhood.

✦ **CREATE A SOURCE FOR COUPONS.** Want even more people to trade with? How about making a "Take a Coupon, Leave a Coupon" box? Set it up at your office, or ask your library, church, or a local cafe if you can place one there. Everyone leaves coupons they can't use, and takes what they can. You'll love stopping by to see what you can get your hands on.

✦ **USE REGIONAL DIFFERENCES TO YOUR ADVANTAGE.** Different coupons are offered to different parts of the country, thanks to regional differences in competition and demand. Because of this, lots of online trading groups have sprung up, with experienced couponers looking for just the right coupon to get them the best price. Log on to HotCouponWorld.com or CouponForum.com to find hundreds of people looking for trades like free Advil coupons in exchange for some high-value coupons on Glad-brand bags. Make sure to check out our Couponing Glossary at the end of this book so you known the terminology!

✦ **GO STRAIGHT TO THE SOURCE.** If there is a name-brand product you use regularly, but you can never seem to find coupons for it, try visiting the company's website directly. Most products list a website on their packaging, but if they don't, try typing the name of the product and the word "coupon" into a search engine. Also make sure to check out WhoKnewTips.com/ExtremeCoupons for a list of companies and brands that offer coupons on their site.

✦ **IT NEVER HURTS TO ASK.** Even if they don't offer free online coupons, many companies have printed coupons that their marketing department keeps for public relations and promotional purposes. An easy and often effective way to get coupons is to write to companies directly (by "real" mail or email—both addresses can usually be found on the product's packaging or its website). This usually works best if you ask for coupons for a specific product, especially if it's brand new to the market. The best thing about these coupons is that they often don't have any restrictions, meaning you can use them with other manufacturer coupons! Find contact information on the product's packaging or their website. We suggest you send mail "Attention: Marketing/PR," and write in the subject heading of your email "Coupon request." Here is an

easy letter or email you can copy and send directly to the company:

Dear [Name of Company],

I love your [kind of product – for example: tortillas, pretzels, frozen dinners], but am having trouble finding coupons for it. Since my family is on a budget, I try to only buy products that I have a coupon for. I was wondering if you would be able to send me coupons for this or any other products you offer discounts on. Thank you so much!

Sincerely,
[Your name]
[Your email address]
[Your mailing address]

EXTREME TIP

Reality show producers love it when extreme couponers go dumpster-diving, but it reality it doesn't happen very often (and is frowned upon by the Coupon Information Corporation, or CIC). However, if you live in an apartment with easy access to your building's recycling bin, it's not a bad idea to take a peek to see if you find extra coupon inserts. Also keep an eye out for newspapers at your workplace or elsewhere whose coupon inserts may be up for grabs.

CHAPTER 3

When and Where to Shop

As you may have discovered, clipping and collecting coupons is kind of like arts and crafts for grown-ups! But all the cutting and saving is nowhere near as much fun as actually getting to use them to save money! When and where you use your coupons is just as important as having a lot of coupons, so make sure to use them wisely. Here's how to know when it's time to take that shopping trip you've been dreaming of—and where it should take place to save the most money.

When to Shop

Depending on whether you're just getting started with couponing or are an old pro, when you decide to take the plunge and use all those coupons you've been saving can be at different times. If you're new to couponing, we recommend going shopping once you have so many coupons you're excited about going! (Isn't the fact that you actually want to go grocery shopping amazing enough to make couponing worthwhile?) This first trip to the store with your coupon stash on-hand will give you the momentum you need to keep up your couponing habit. Make sure to circle the "Amount you saved" total on your receipt and tack it up to your refrigerator for inspiration!

If you're a more experienced couponer, you may have begun to get a sense of the lowest price you can get for a certain item—in fact, many extreme couponers start lists of the most common items they buy and the lowest price they ever paid for it. But whether you're a newbie or a seasoned vet, there are few principles of shopping with coupons to live by.

MATCHUPS

Knowing the best time to shop is all about one thing: matchups! "Matchup" is couponer slang for when a coupon you have matches up with an in-store sale or other coupons. If you're a more casual couponer, the easiest way to go about finding matchups is simply to check out your store's circular once you get there (check near the door or at the customer service desk). Bring along an accordion file or envelope-system full of your coupons (see Chapter 6: Organizing Your Coupons and Stockpile for more ideas), and see if any of them align with the sales that are currently going on.

To get all of your groceries and home items at the lowest price possible at all times, a little more advance planning is required. It's best to take a look at the circulars of several stores before you go, to make sure you're getting the best deal possible. But don't worry! It's much

easier than you think. Couponers around the US have gathered together to share their frugal finds, and finding what coupons will match up with which stores is as easy as visiting a couponing blog each week.

Check out some of the coupon matchup sites at WhoKnewTips.com/ExtremeCoupons, and you'll immediately see how easy it is to save half off and more on just about everything you buy. For instance, if you shop regularly at Kroger, head over to StockpilingMoms.com/category/kroger. There, you'll find the current week's sales at the store, as well as a list of recent coupons that have been offered for the sale products. Get the coupons by following their links, or get them from your own stockpile. We've listed all the major grocery chains at WhoKnewTips.com/ExtremeCoupons.

WHO KNEW?

When looking at your store's circular, be aware that not all of the products they show are on sale (even if they say "Deal!"). Stores often advertise a product just to call attention to it (like if they have too many in stock), not because it's on sale. So before you snatch up what you think is a deal, make sure to consider the prices of similar items.

BUY NOW!

With all the excitement of watching your coupons add up, you might begin to wonder, "When do I know when to go buy something?" While having one coupon for an item is great, extreme couponers usually make sure they are getting the lowest possible price for an item by stacking up several coupons and a sale. But what is that price? Here are a few times you should definitely buy:

✦ **YOU HAVE AN OVERAGE.** An "overage" is when the total value of your coupons is actually higher than the sale price of an item. Ding, ding, ding! As if you needed us to tell you, overages are the best times to buy! Most stores will not give you actual cash back for overages, but some stores will give you a store credit. Otherwise, you'll have to buy more items (basically getting them for free) to cover the overage.

✦ **YOU CAN'T BEAT THE PRICE.** Later on, we'll talk about some strategies for tracking your store's sale cycle to figure out at what time each year products are at their cheapest. But a good rule of thumb when you're beginning to coupon is to buy the item if you can get it for 50 percent off its usual price. If it's 75 percent off or more, consider it a bargain worthy of stockpiling!

✦ **"BUY ONE, GET ONE FREE" SALES.** These promotions are so exciting to deal-lovers that they have their own acronym: BOGO. The reason why they're so thrilling? Because you can usually use manufacturer coupons for the item you're getting for free! For instance, your CVS is having a BOGO sale on Pantene shampoo, and you found a 50¢ off coupon online. Print it out twice, then take both coupons to the store and use them to get $1 off your BOGO purchase!

✦ **YOUR COUPONS ARE ABOUT TO EXPIRE.** If you've been saving your coupons in an attempt to get a lower price on a particular item, but your coupons are about to expire, go for it now before it's too late. You may be able to get a better price later, but getting a few at the current discount price is never a bad idea, especially since it's more fun to be rewarded for your coupon-saving savvy.

EXTREME TIP

If you have a ton of coupons for something and are afraid it's going to sell out before you get to the store, call ahead and ask the manager if the store would be willing to special order a large quantity and hold it for you. Make sure you get the manager's name, and ask when you should come pick it up. They usually won't even have you prepay before you come get it!

KNOW WHEN TO GO

The most important rule of grocery shopping? Never go to the grocery store on an empty stomach. If you're hungry, you'll not only want to rush through shopping (taking less time to compare unit prices), but you'll make more impulse purchases because everything looks so tasty! Go right after breakfast, lunch, or a snack and you won't be tempted. Late morning and early afternoon are also great times to shop because the store won't be as crowded.

You should also try to make your shopping trip as big as possible, rather than taking several small trips. Not only will you save on gas money, but according to a study by the Marketing Science Institute, shoppers who are only making a quick trip to the store purchase an average of 54 percent more than they had planned. In other words, plan out your trip and take your time, and you'll be much more likely to save.

WHO KNEW?

Couponing and discount-hunting works best when you can focus on it, and that means it's much easier if you don't have your kids with you. If their other parent isn't available to watch them, try trading off with a friend: One of you goes shopping while the other watches all the kids, then the other goes

for a shopping trip and picks up the kids on the way home. If you have to take the kids along (as so many of us must!), bring along something to keep them entertained in the cart. If that doesn't work, buy them a special snack like Goldfish or animal crackers, and let them eat it while you shop!

EXTREME TIP

If you're planning on using a boatload of coupons, you may want to plan your grocery trips when the store manager is on duty. (Check to see if there is a sign that lists his or her hours by the customer service desk, or ask an employee.) That way, if you encounter any problems when your coupons are being rung up, the person in charge will be available to speak to you.

Where to Shop

There used to be a horrible grocery store a couple of miles away from us. The selection was bad, the aisles were so narrow that you had to say "excuse me" (or "sorry my kid just did that") every 2 feet, and the parking lot was a nightmare. But their sales were always better, and we found that they still had sale items available— unlike our other local supermarket, whose sale section often resembled a deserted wasteland.

Unfortunately, even if one store is much nicer to shop at, you need to shop at the store that has the best deals—and to maximize your savings, you'll probably have to shop at more than one store. Keep an eye on all local stores' circulars, and see which ones match up to the coupons you have on hand. Compare the stores' regular prices too—look at the receipts from shopping trips side-by-side and you should easily be able to see if one store is much more expensive than the other. Also keep in mind that some departments may be cheaper than others. For instance, one store might have less expensive produce, while the other has better deals in their bakery. Keep lists and check them twice!

EXTREME TIP

Save gas, let your babysitting dollars go further, and get more rush out of your extreme couponing trip by visiting two supermarkets one after the other. Keep a cooler in the truck of your car to keep frozen and chilled items cool until you get home. You can also store fragile items like eggs in the cooler, so they don't roll around in your trunk and break.

PICKING THE BEST STORE

Choosing the right supermarket can impact your coupon savings just as much as how many coupons you've collected. That's because each store has different guidelines and restrictions for coupons. Stop by your store's customer service desk and ask about their coupon policy, or visit the store's website to see what their restrictions are. Some questions to ask are:

✦ **WHAT IS THE STORE'S POLICY ABOUT INTERNET COUPONS?** Some stores won't allow you to use two of the same internet coupon on the same item (even if no restrictions are printed on it), and other stores don't allow coupons printed from the internet at all!

✦ **WILL THE STORE GIVE YOU CREDIT FOR OVERAGES?** If you have coupons totaling a dollar off and the item is only 95¢, will the remaining 5¢ be given to you as cash or store credit, applied to your shopping trip's balance (i.e., you would have to buy something other than just that item to have your 5¢ credited), or not counted at all?

✦ **DOES THE STORE PRICE-MATCH OTHER ADS?** Some stores will match the advertised price of the same item from another store. Find out if yours does!

✦ **IS THERE A PER-ITEM COUPON LIMIT?** Not all stores are as well-versed in coupon restrictions and guidelines as they should be. Even if your coupon doesn't have any restrictions printed on it, some stores may not allow you to use two of the same coupon for one item. It's also important to ask if you can buy multiple items and use multiple coupons if they say "limit one per purchase." While most stores allow this, you'll find that oftentimes the cashier doesn't. Make sure you know the store's policy before you go so that if your cashier tells you using multiple coupons isn't allowed, you can kindly tell him that isn't true. (The next chapter, At the Store, gives you more tips on what to do if your coupons get rejected at the register.)

✦ **DOES THE STORE HAVE ANY "SPECIAL" DAYS FOR DISCOUNTS?** Lots of stores have a day each week that's reserved for different kinds of discounts. If you are a senior or a member of a military family, make sure to find out if there is a day where you get extra savings while you shop. Some stores also have events each week or month where they double (or even triple!) coupons.

✦ **WHAT OTHER DISCOUNTS DOES THE STORE OFFER?** Competition for customers is tough these days, and stores usually offer small perks to make sure you come

back. Does your store give you a few cents back if you use a reusable grocery bag? Do they offer store credit for transferring prescriptions to their pharmacy or taking a short survey that appears on your receipt? These programs can mean easy savings for you, so make sure you know about everything that's available.

✦ **DOES THE STORE REGULARLY DOUBLE COUPONS?**
They're few and far between these days, but if you can find a store that always doubles the value of your coupons (that is, give you $1 off for a 50¢-off coupon), you've hit the couponer's jackpot.

EXTREME TIP

Print out a copy of the store's coupon policy off their website, or ask at the customer service counter for a printed-out copy. That way, if you run in to any problems when you're checking out, you'll have the policy with you to show the cashier.

COUPON DOUBLING:
WHAT YOU NEED TO KNOW

Your grocery store has said the magic words: "We double." But before you call up *Extreme Couponing* and tell them you're about to make the grocery shopping trip of a lifetime, make sure you know the store's

restrictions on doubling. Most stores will only double coupons up to a certain monetary limit, like $1. That means that if your coupon says 25¢ off, you'll get 50¢ off instead; but if your coupon says 75¢ off you'll only get $1 off. If your coupon is worth $1 or more, it won't be doubled.

Some supermarkets have even more specific rules. For instance, a store might tell you that you can only double three cereal coupons per trip; or that coupon doubling for produce is off-limits entirely. Some stores won't double internet coupons, while others will only allow you to double a particular coupon once, even if you have several copies of it. Find out what your store's policy is and make sure to factor this in to your shopping trip.

Unfortunately, just because your store doubles doesn't necessarily mean it's the cheapest option. Because stores know that some people specifically seek-out coupon-doubling stores, they'll allow it in their policy—but then jack up the prices on the most commonly couponed items. Do a price comparison among local stores to make sure the price hike isn't more than the value of the coupon!

WHO KNEW?

Visit Couponing.about.com/od/groceryzone/a/
doublecoupons.htm for a reader-generated list of
stores that double coupons. And if you find one near
you, consider yourself lucky!

BEYOND GROCERY STORES

When hunting for the best prices, don't let your journey
stop at the supermarket. Sometimes, stores that don't
specialize in groceries will actually give you the lowest
price on some staples. For instance, a nearby gas station
or convenience store might have a special price on milk
or soda to get customers inside. CVS, Walgreens, and
other drug stores are also good places to buy certain
foods, such as soup, spaghetti sauce, and candy. Make
sure to take a walk down these stores' food aisles
and compare the prices to your regular supermarket,
especially the food that's on sale. Another great place
to find low prices on food is at your local dollar store.

As long as they're chains, most of these stores will
take coupons. But sometimes, the lowest price can be
found even without a coupon discount. If you live in
an urban area, independently-owned ethnic markets
usually have rock-bottom prices on staples native to that
country, like tortillas, rice, and spices. Wholesale clubs

like Costco and Sam's Club are also prime examples of stores that don't take coupons, but will give you such a discount that it doesn't matter (BJ's is currently the only wholesale club that takes coupons).

And just like everything else these days, sometimes the cheapest place to find groceries is online. This is also a great option if you don't have a car to haul big loads of groceries home! Some of our favorite sites for buying in bulk online are Yourgrocer.com, Meijer.com, and MyBrands.com. Amazon.com also sells some grocery products. For a list of other sites that sell groceries and household items, visit SmartLifeBlog.com/100-places-to-buy-your-groceries-online.

WHO KNEW?

Just because you don't belong to a wholesale club doesn't necessarily mean you can't shop there. Many states have laws that say that a store must allow anyone (even non-members) to buy prescription medication and/or alcohol there. Most stores will also allow you to shop there if a friend has given you a gift card for the store. Call the store's customer service department and ask them what their policy is.

CHAPTER 4

At the Store

Y ou've been clipping coupons for weeks, have picked out the best store for your bargain hunt, and you even managed to line up a few sales with the coupons you have on-hand. It's time to go shopping! Even if you haven't enlisted your eight-year-old to follow you around with a video camera so you can pretend you're on TV, it can still be pretty exciting to find the item you have several coupons for and know you're going to get at a great cost. We call it our "supermarket treasure hunt," and can usually get the kids to help us find the items we're looking for. But once you go through the automatic doors and get your cart, it's easy to get overwhelmed. Here's what you need to know while you're at the store.

What to Buy

For everyday shoppers, the answer to "What should I buy?" is "What you need!" But for extreme couponers, purchases have less to do with what they need than what they can get a great deal on. That's because when they find something at a very low price, they buy as many as they can at that price, and keep them for later. When you're just starting to coupon, make sure to start small so your budget can handle it. Cover the things you need to buy before you spend money on your

stockpile. Our only other rule for saving at the grocery store, whether you're using coupons or not? Stick to your list!

MAKING YOUR SHOPPING LIST

If you've taken a look at our "Buy Now!" list in the previous chapter, you know some of the sure signs that you're getting a great deal. The next step is making sure you're taking advantage of it! The easiest way to do this is to make a list. If you're new to couponing, this shopping list will be pretty much like every other shopping list you've ever written—just make sure to indicate which items you have coupons for. You may also want to add the amount of the coupon and whether it's an online or physical coupon.

Once you've started to collect a formidable coupon stockpile, you'll find that your grocery list begins with items you know you can get cheaply. First, take a quick look through your coupon stash to remind yourself of what you've got on hand. Make sure to note any products you can already get for half off or more.

Next, check out your local stores' websites for their sales circular and coupons, or consult one of the many coupon matchup sites we've listed in at WhoKnewTips.com/ExtremeCoupons. See any great

deals, buy-one-get-one-free offers, or (yay!) items you can get for absolutely free because of overages? Add them to your list! You may want to do one last online search for additional coupons for the items you're buying, or hit up some of the company websites we've linked to from our site for even more coupons.

WHO KNEW?

If you love making shopping lists and crunching the numbers of how much you're going to save, you'll love this spreadsheet as seen on TLC's *Extreme Couponing* show: WorkingMomCoupons.com/wmc-couponing-spreadsheet. You have to pay a small fee for it, but you can use it on Excel or the iPad, and for the super-organized, it will be worth it!

Once you've got a master list of all the items you know you can get at a discount, make life a little easier on yourself by rewriting the list in the order your grocery store is laid out. (If you make your list on the computer, this step is even easier because you can just copy and paste the text.) Then stick all the coupons you'll need in an envelope and you're ready to rumble!

In addition to an envelope of coupons you'll need on your trip, many couponers bring their entire coupon

Who Knew? Extreme Coupons

stash to the store with them (even if they leave it in the car). If there's an unadvertised sale or special clearance going on, you know you'll have your coupons at the ready to stack up your savings!

WHO KNEW?

Want to lay out your shopping list the same way as the store, but you're not exactly sure which aisle is where? Check on the store's website or at their in-store customer service counter to see if they have a map of the store available.

EXTREME TIP

The most extreme couponers plan their shopping trip out to the cent, and that means writing down the price you expect to pay for each item next to it on your list. That way, when you see the prices at the store, you'll know if there are any differences and can account for them in your budget. Just make sure to bring a calculator and a pen!

WHAT SIZE TO BUY

If you're used to checking the "unit" prices of items at the grocery store, you know that buying the bigger size almost always means a better value. But when you have coupons, the opposite is usually true. That's because

with couponing, the name of the game is getting the biggest percentage off your purchase. For instance, if you have a $1-off coupon and buy the product that costs $2.00, you're getting half off. But if you buy the product that costs $2.50, you're only getting 40 percent off.

This method can pay off big in your store's trial-size aisle. If your coupon says "any size" (and doesn't exclude trial sizes), you'll often find that you can get 60–95 percent off your purchase when you buy a trial size. Buy several trial sizes with several coupons and you have the same amount of product as you would with a regular size—at a fraction of the cost.

EXTREME TIP

Coupon barcodes don't always tell the computer the same thing that's written on the coupon in terms of product types and quantity limits—and some extreme couponers have used this to their advantage by learning how to "read" the barcodes on the coupons to get a better deal. While some stores abide by the "if the computer takes it, you can use it" rule, many couponers feel that knowingly using a coupon in a way the manufacturer didn't intend is unethical and gives couponers a bad name. For more information about how to read your coupon's barcode, check out P4P.amesnjas.com/tutorials/barcode-basics.

HOW MANY TO BUY

Unless you're really trying to get on TV, you probably haven't called ahead to pre-order 50 pallets of those Kit-Kats that are on sale for you haul away in your semi-truck. So once you've found the item you're looking for in the store, how do you know how many to buy? If your savings are coupon-based, the answer may be as easy as buying as many as you have coupons for. But if you're able to clip dozens of coupons, or the discount is all due to sales, the solution may not be so easy.

Many avid couponers will stock up on a six month's supply of an item if they feel they're getting it at the lowest price possible. Others don't have as much room to stockpile—they may want to buy only one or two months' worth, or only as much as they think they'll need until the next sale (in the next chapter, Secrets about Sales and Loyalty Programs, we'll give you more information about figuring out when the next sale might be). One thing is for certain, though—buying every single one of the discounted products is considered rude by others hoping to score deals at that store. Known as "shelf-clearing," it's the scourge of every couponer who has found a store that doubles coupons or often has great sales! Luckily, if you're the victim of a shelf-clearer who got to the store before you, there's still hope: When you get to the cashier, explain that they're

out of the item and ask for a rain check. Most stores will give you a voucher that allows you to get the discount price of the item once it's back in stock. Just make sure to check the expiration date, if there is one.

WHO KNEW?

Don't miss out on even more savings while you're at the grocery store. Make sure to keep an eye out for those blinkies, peelies, and tear-pads as you're going down the aisle. You may also want to ask at the customer service desk and pharmacy counter if they have any coupons.

WHAT NOT TO BUY

Remember...as fun as they are, coupons don't actually save you money if you're buying a product you wouldn't normally buy, or are buying a higher quantity than you will ever use. Also make sure to check generic and other brands to see if they are still cheaper than the product you have a coupon for! A coupon that saves you 30¢ isn't much good if the item is 40¢ more expensive than the store brand.

When you're checking out prices at the store, take a look at the lowest shelf first and work your way up. You'll find that the highest prices are at eye level—since that's where people in a hurry will most likely grab a

product from. When comparing prices around the store, make sure you look farther than just up or down. Similar products may shelved in different parts of the store. For instance, cheese can usually be found near the dairy section, in a "gourmet" section, and at the deli counter. Because of different sales and promotions, you never know where you'll find it for cheapest.

The ends of aisles are also prime places to find unadvertised clearance items from around the store. Just be aware—sometimes the higher-priced brands actually pay the store for good placement, which means these items are might be priced much higher!

EXTREME TIP

Want to make sure you're getting the absolute lowest price on everything in the store before you take that big trip (you know, the one where you scan the receipt and post it on your Facebook page)? Take a quick trip to the store the day before. Make sure any overage items you're planning on buying are in stock and that you're aware of any unadvertised sales going on. That way, you'll be sure your savings are at their maximum!

At the Register

It's the moment of truth—you're at the register with a wad of coupons, ready to watch the numbers come off your total. But before you get to the finish line, there are a few hurdles you'll have to get through. There are also opportunities for even more savings, so get your game face on and head for the front of the store.

CHOOSING A CHECK-OUT LINE

Store cashiers will react in all different ways if you pay for more than half your purchase with coupons. Most will think it's fun, and will even be impressed with your coupon-clipping skills. Some, however, are not as friendly as others. They may think you're trying to scam the store, or will be unsure about coupon policies. Extreme couponers will often talk about "cashier profiling"—looking for the most cheerful employee, or the one they think will happily override something when the computer beeps. But we think the best advice is simply to find a cashier you like and try to go to his or her check-out line if available.

When you approach the cashier, you should tell them right away that you have lots and lots of coupons, so they know it's going to take a while to ring you up! They may even want to close the check-out line behind

you. If you have multiples of coupons that say "one per order" or "one per transaction," ask if it's OK if you break your purchase into multiple transactions. You should also know that most store computers have a maximum number of items they can ring up in each transaction, so if you have more than 200 items, you may also have to break up your purchase.

Make sure you watch carefully as you're being rung up. A recent study found that 10 percent of items at supermarkets are scanned in at the incorrect price—and often coupons are, too. When you get up to the checkout line, it's a good idea to take your stack of coupons and layer them so that similar coupons are not near each other, and that the coupons you printed out from the internet are interspersed throughout. This way, you'll ensure that they don't stick together when the cashier is quickly scanning each one in the pile.

WHO KNEW?

Sometimes (especially for free product coupons), the cashier has to write the retail price of the item on the coupon. If you have any of these coupons, you'll do the cashier a favor by putting these items at the end of the conveyer belt, so she doesn't have to scan through a long receipt to find the price. We also try to put these coupons together so the cashier only has to get out her pen once!

WHEN CHECKOUTS GO WRONG

As fun as extreme couponing can be, sometimes when you're walking around the store with ten tubes of toothpaste and fifty boxes of cereal in your cart, you can feel a bit like a freak. So when a cashier tells you they're going to have to call a manager over to talk to you just because you're trying to use a lot of coupons, it can be hard not to get mad. *Don't get mad.* Whether he's new at the job, not familiar with coupon language, or just making sure he covers his butt, the cashier will almost always call over the manager if you're using a ton of coupons, especially if you end up with an overage or the cashier has to enter any of the coupons manually.

You'll usually find that if there's an issue, the cashier will call over the manager and the manager will fix it and be happy you're shopping there (stores get paid for manufacturer coupons, so they aren't losing any money!). But occasionally, we've had cashiers simply tell us we can't use certain coupons when we think we should be able to. Here's what to do when the store doesn't want to take your coupons:

✦ **BE NICE.** Remember, the people working at the store are just trying to do their jobs. They're usually glad to help you, especially if you're friendly and patient.

✦ **ASK QUESTIONS.** Before you get defensive, ask why the coupon isn't accepted. You may find that the cashier is simply confused about the store's policy or the wording on coupons. One thing we hear a lot is, "This coupon says one per purchase, and you have five of them." When this happens, you'll have to explain that buying five of the item means that there's five purchases, and the computer wouldn't take them otherwise. Whether it's this issue or another, they can often be easily resolved with some polite explaining.

✦ **REFER BACK TO THE STORE'S POLICY.** If the cashier sticks to his guns about not accepting the coupon, ask if you can see a copy of the store's coupon policy—or better yet, get a copy of their policy ahead of time from the customer service desk or the store's website, and bring it along with you. Point out the section of the coupon policy that backs you up that the coupon should be accepted and gently explain why.

✦ **DON'T BE AFRAID TO TALK TO THE MANGER.** If you still think you should be allowed to use the coupon, but the cashier won't budge, don't be afraid to talk to the manager. The manager will usually be more familiar with the policy, and will either be able to better explain it, or will allow the coupon.

✦ **YOU WIN SOME, YOU LOSE SOME.** Even if your coupon is ultimately not accepted, remember that you can always try to use it elsewhere. Not buying the item at this store also lets them know that they've lost a sale because they wouldn't accept your coupon. Take your defeat gracefully, but write a letter or email to the store's corporate office (you can usually find the address on their website) explaining what happened and why you think you were in the right. You never know when you might change the store's (written or unwritten) policy, or get a free coupon for your trouble.

CATALINA COUPONS

While you're at the checkout, make sure to keep an eye out for Catalina coupons. No, they're not coupons from a Caribbean island…they're coupons from the Catalina Marketing Association that print up from a machine near the register. You've probably been handed one or two of these coupons with your receipt before, and if you're ever wondered if there was a rhyme or reason to it, here's what you've wanted to know!

Catalina coupons are printed based on what you've purchased. Most often, they're for money off a product (either from a brand that you purchased or its competitors), and depending on the store's coupon

policy, you can sometimes even use these coupons at other stores. The other kind of Catalina coupon you'll come across is for an amount off a future purchase. These types are usually store-specific, and can sometimes be for $5 off or more!

No matter which kind of Catalina deal it is, it can be impossible to predict what coupons will print out. The Catalina company does release some information about them at CouponNetwork.com/yourbucks-catalina-coupons, but there are also many unlisted deals to be had. Luckily, you can find a list of the Catalinas being offered at a wide variety of supermarkets at LivingRichWithCoupons.com/catalina-deals-2. Plan carefully, because if you receive Catalina coupons with your purchase, most stores will allow you to make a second purchase to use them right then and there.

EXTREME TIP

If you're using the maximum number of coupons allowed by your store on each item, also using a Catalina coupon will put you over your limit. Depending on the value of the coupon, you may find it's worth it to buy one or two low-priced items (like gum) so that they can be accepted. Or, buy items that are usually hard to find coupons for, like meat and produce.

CHAPTER 5

The Secrets about Sales and Loyalty Programs

As you've begun to see, there's a second side to the couponing coin, and that's sales. Lining up store sales with available coupons is essential for getting rock-bottom prices on everything you buy—and it's what really made us feel like the time we spent on couponing was worth the savings.

Luckily, it's much easier than you might think to stack coupons on top of sales. Any of the almost 200 coupon matchup sites listed at WhoKnewTips.com/ExtremeCoupons will tell you what's on sale at your local grocery stores, as well as what recent coupons have been offered—including links to currently available online coupons. It's also fairly easy to figure out when items will be on sale at your local store.

WHO KNEW?

Grocery stores plan their sales carefully with the manufacturer—in fact, many store sales are paid for by the manufacturers themselves. Therefore, it's not uncommon for a coupon to come out about 2–6 weeks before a sale. The manufacturer figures you'll buy it once with a coupon, then find it on sale and buy it again (and then you'll be hooked!). By saving your coupons to use when an item is on sale, you'll save twice as much, then move on to whatever you can get for mere pennies next time.

Deciphering Sales

Before we move on to matching up sales and store loyalty programs, it's important to make sure you understand exactly what the sale is offering. Marketers often use vague language on purpose, so sometimes you will even have to ask the store to clarify. Here are a few tips to remember.

SALE STACKING:
KNOW WHAT YOU'RE GETTING

Stores will often discount an item, then discount it again. But before you grab something because you think it's half the price, you should know that that's usually not the case. For example, when something is offered for 25 percent off, with an additional 25 percent taken at the register, you're usually not actually getting 50 percent off—you're getting 25 percent of 25 percent—or 43.75 percent off. This is a tactic that is commonly used in the clearance section of stores.

SPEAK THE STORE'S LANGUAGE

Your store says avocados are 5 for $10...does that mean that you have to buy five to get them at that price, or that avocados are priced at $2 each? At most

stores, it's usually the latter. Take a close look and see if the advertisement or sign says "separate price" or "individual price" and then a different amount. If that's the case, you have to buy them all to get the deal. Otherwise, you probably only have to buy one. If the ad is unclear, ask your store. If they phrase it "buy 2 for $1" and you only have to buy one, chances are that's always the case, so you won't have to ask your store each time.

WHO KNEW?

Marketing language is at it again. Make sure that when your store flyer says "buy one, get one free," that the item is not actually 50 percent off, regardless of whether you buy one or twenty. Since the savings is the same, many stores will phrase the sale in this way to get people to buy more than one item.

The Sales Cycle

Now that you know some of the tricks stores employ with the wording of their sales offers, you can maximize your savings every time there's a sale. But how do you know when the stuff you want is going to be discounted? Believe it or not, there's a particular formula for it, and it's easy to learn. Each store plans promotions on various items in a cycle. So if you can monitor the cycle, you'll know when items are going to be on sale.

TRACKING SALES

Figuring out your store's sale cycle may take some effort, but once you've done the work, you won't have to do it again (unless you move!)—and you will be saving yourself thousands per year. Basically, what you have to do is keep track of items you regularly by, and write down when they're on sale (and how much they're on sale for). Once you've kept track for six months or so, you'll begin to see a pattern: most stores change what is on sale every 4–6 weeks. The more you track this pattern, the more easily you'll be able to predict what's on sale.

How you decide to track your store's sales is up to you. Here's what you need to know about each method of making a price list:

✦ **PENCIL AND PAPER.** Whether you use a small notebook or a piece of printer paper, some people find keeping track of prices by hand is easiest for them. It's as simple as writing down the items you buy and how much you bought them for. Organize it by store or by item. Some great printable templates can be found at MomsBudget.com/printables/groceryprintables.html.

✦ **ON THE COMPUTER.** Many people find that editing their list on the computer is easier, and a spreadsheet

program like Microsoft Excel is perfect for the job. Newer versions of Excel already include a "grocery list" template (or you can search for the template on the Office.com site). Or download a price book template at NCNBlog.com/wp-content/uploads/2007/11/grocerypricebook.xls. If you don't have Excel or a similar program, check out Docs.google.com/spreadsheets. It's an internet-based spreadsheet-maker from Google that has all the same basic features as Excel, plus it gives you the ability to easily share with others.

✦ **ON YOUR MOBILE DEVICE.** If you have an iPhone, Android, or other smartphone, you know that sometimes it's just easier (and more fun) to keep track of things using it, and price lists are no exception. This is our favorite method of tracking prices because we can get our boys to help if they get to do it on the iPhone! For iPhones, our favorite app is SHOPare; for Android, try Price Book BD.

EXTREME TIP

If you plan out weekly menu plans for your family's meals, use your price list and menu plan together to make sure you're planning your meals around what's on sale!

SEASONAL SALES YOU CAN COUNT ON

Sales cycles vary from store to store, which is why you have to keep track of your own store's cycle to see the most savings. But there are some seasonal sales you can count on to happen each year in the US. Here they are, broken down by month.

✦ **JANUARY.** Post-holiday items like candy, turkey, ham, and stuffing; diet foods like low-calorie frozen meals and snacks; oatmeal; Super Bowl foods like chips and soda.

✦ **FEBRUARY.** Dog food; waffles; condoms and other family planning products (before Valentine's Day); candy (after Valentine's Day); canned vegetables and tuna.

✦ **MARCH.** Frozen foods including pizza and ice cream; cleaning products; paper products like paper towels and plates; Cajun seasonings and mixes (in celebration of Mardi Gras).

✦ **APRIL.** After-Easter items such as baking supplies, candy, ham, and eggs; Earth Day items like reusable tote bags and organic foods; olive oil; butter; post-Passover items like matzo, potatoes, and coconut flakes.

✦ **MAY.** Pet food, treats, and toys; sunscreen and bug spray; picnic items like condiments (ketchup, barbecue sauce, etc.), hot dogs, ground beef, soda, buns, and plastic forks; Cinco de Mayo promotions like salsa, tortillas, and taco shells; car wash and maintenance items.

✦ **JUNE.** Dairy products; produce; salad dressing; pre–Fourth of July sales on charcoal and other supplies.

✦ **JULY.** Post–Fourth of July sales on charcoal, hot dogs, ground beef, buns, and picnic supplies; produce; bottled water and soda; school supplies.

✦ **AUGUST.** Cleaning items; dorm room and school supplies; lunch meat, Jell-O cups, and other lunchbox essentials; produce; kids' summer toys, as well as fans, pool-cleaning equipment, and anything else summer-related.

✦ **SEPTEMBER.** Cereal; canned goods (especially tomato products); baby products; produce.

✦ **OCTOBER.** Seafood; pie shells and filling; premade foods like macaroni and cheese and pizza; dog food; produce; safety equipment like smoke alarms.

✦ **NOVEMBER.** Candy; baking products including chocolate chips, cake mixes, and nuts; coffee and tea; soup and broth; Thanksgiving foods like stuffing, instant potatoes, and gravy mix.

✦ **DECEMBER.** Baking products; pasta and tomato sauce; turkeys (after Thanksgiving and Christmas); crackers; canned goods; oranges and grapefruit; toys; cold remedies and other medicine; toothbrushes; vitamins.

WHO KNEW?

When it comes to yearly sales, holidays play a big role. Prices for traditional holiday foods and supplies will go down before the big event, because stores like to publicize sales for items they know people need. After the holiday, however, is when you'll see the rock bottom prices for everything—if there's anything left. We usually buy some before and some after the holiday, depending on how our coupons line up.

Working Your Store's Loyalty Program

Google "shop for free" and you'll get more than 3 million hits. Store loyalty programs are what making shopping for free possible. While just about all supermarkets have loyalty programs that will get you discounts on items (and yet another tiny card on your key ring), drugstore loyalty programs, which offer "cash back" as a reward, are the ones that you'll find the most fruitful.

WHO KNEW?

Coupons and cash-back offers that are printed up as a result of your loyalty card are usually linked to that card. So to get the deal, you have to have your card with you! This also means that you can't give these kinds of coupons to your friends to use.

DRUGSTORE PAYDAY

Even better than shopping for free is when you can get paid to shop, and by working your drugstore's loyalty program, you can walk out of the store with more money to spend there than when you walked in. This is possible because you may receive, for instance, a $2-off "cash back" coupon for buying a $2 item that you have a 50¢-off coupon for. In other words, you'd be making 50¢!

At most drugstores, there are two different times you'll get these cash-back coupons: for purchasing specific items, and for spending a certain amount of money. Stack them each time you shop and you'll basically never have to pay for a trip to the drugstore again. For instance, during a recent week at Walgreens, shoppers could receive 50¢ to $2 back on several different products in the store. You could also get a $5 cash-back "Register Reward" when you spent $25 in the store. By buying $25 worth of the products with individual cash-back offers, the dollar amount of the Register Rewards we received was over $30, yet we only spent $19.50 after coupons.

Sometimes, you may even want to buy items you don't want and give them away, just to get the cash-back coupons. For instance, if you have a manufacturer coupon for a free $5 package of hair dye, and can receive $5 in cash-back coupons for buying it, figure out what color your best friend uses, pronto! She'll get the hair dye, and you'll have $5 off your next transaction.

Like all extreme couponing, the secret to being successful at drugstore payday is knowing what's on sale before you go. You'll also have to know about the rules and limitations of each chain's program. Make sure to visit the websites of CVS, Walgreens, or your local store to find out more.

WHO KNEW?

Don't have a friend who needs that hair dye you bought just for the coupons? There are still lots of organizations that can use commonly on-sale items like toothpaste, diabetes meters, and yes, even hair dye. Nursing homes, women's shelters, church organizations, and anyone having a garage sale are great places to start.

EXTREME TIP

It's important to know that just about every drugstore will allow you to make two or more transactions, in order to use a cash-back coupon you just earned on your previous transaction. Just make sure you buy all the items in the right order, so that you receive cash-back coupons from your first transaction to buy the items in the second, etc.

CHAPTER 6

Organizing Your Coupons and Stockpile

We'll admit it: The phrase "Get organized!" often sends chills down our spines. But being organized is essential for sticking with couponing—even a couple of weeks of leaving printed-out coupons in a pile and not organizing your inserts will have you looking at the mess and wondering if couponing is worthwhile. And when it comes to your "shopping at home" stockpile...well, let's just say we're less a lot less organized than a supermarket, and it took some time before we were able to use our messy stockpile to its fullest. Do what we say, and not as we do, and you'll be able to easily organize your couponing efforts.

WHO KNEW?

The big secret to our couponing success? The TV. By devoting a few of our many hours spent in front of the TV each week to couponing, we not only always find the time to organize our stash, we even look forward to it!

Organizing Your Coupons

There are a lot of different ways to organize coupons, and which one is the "best" is up to you. The most important thing to remember is that only you (and—if you're lucky!—your spouse) will be using your system, so

don't second-guess what works for you. Some people find sorting their coupons by category (dairy, cereal, snacks, etc.) easiest, while others prefer to sort their coupons according to how the store is laid out. You can also sort them by brand, expiration date, alphabetically, or anything else that makes sense to you—if you are going to remember that coupon for Kraft American cheese as "Kraft," rather than "Cheese," then set up your organization system to reflect that. To help you decide how you'd like to organize these categories, we've outlined the different types of coupon organization systems below, along with their pros and cons.

WHO KNEW?

No matter what kind of organization system you use, you'll have to periodically go through and get rid of expired coupons. The good news is that you don't have throw them away! Supermarkets on overseas military bases, as a matter of policy, accept expired coupons; and the Overseas Coupon Program will let you "adopt" a base full of personnel to send your expired coupons to! Just go to OCPnet.org and click on "Base list" to find a base that needs coupons, then click on "Adoption form" to adopt them. Then, send your coupons that are up to two months past their expiration date to the address provided. Postage is no more than it would be to mail something within the United States.

EXTREME TIP

As you're sorting your coupons, keep an eye out for coupons that ask you to write your name and address on them. Writing down your info will almost always lead to more coupons in the mail, so do it now before you forget to do it in the check-out line!

ENVELOPES

This no-frills method may be one of the most popular for organizing coupons. Just grab a bunch of envelopes, write whatever categories you're using on the front, and put the coupons inside. If you have multiple coupons for the same item, keep them together with paper clips. It's that easy!

✦ **PROS.** This method is super easy and inexpensive— you can even use business reply and other envelopes that come with your bills. It's also easily portable, so you can take your coupon collection with you to the store.

✦ **CONS.** While the envelope method is great for beginners, most extreme couponers quickly outgrow it because it's hard to see all your coupons at once, and those envelopes don't hold as many coupons as you'd think!

COUPON BINDERS

It seems like just about every extreme couponer on TV has a giant coupon binder (or five), and it's not just because it's fun to show off all your coupons one-by-one. Using a coupon binder is probably the most streamlined way to sort and organize your coupons.

✦ **PROS.** If you love being super-organized, this is probably the method for you. It's great to be able to see each one of your coupons and to easily flip through them. It's especially effortless to weed out expired coupons, and since you're seeing your coupons all the time, you'll be able to more easily remember what coupons you have. While a coupon binder isn't as portable as some of the other methods, it's still simple enough to keep it in your car or cart while you're in the store, in case there's a sale you didn't know about. Keep all the coupons you plan on using in a separate envelope.

✦ **CONS.** The amount of clipping and organization that goes into a coupon binder makes it the most time-consuming of your options. It can also get expensive—you'll need a very sturdy binder (most couponers go with the zippered variety so that the coupons never

fall out), as well tabbed pages for category names. Finding the appropriate holders for your coupons can also be a challenge. Some sites sell plastic sheets just for coupons, while other couponers swear by a combination of baseball card, photo, and business card holders. No matter what you choose, it can be hard to make sure all your coupons fit in the slots and are visible.

EXTREME TIP

If you use a coupon binder, you'll probably want to include some full-sized pouches in addition to baseball card holders. Our inexpensive alternative? Take a sturdy Ziploc bag with a zipper closure and three-hole punch it on the sealed end. Place it in your binder for an instant coupon pouch!

COUPON WALLETS

Looking for something a little fancier than envelopes, but you're not ready to go full-on coupon binder yet? Coupon wallets are a great in-between option with some added benefits. Buy a check-sized expanding file from an office supply store for $5–$10, or you may opt for one of the many "coupon clutches" now available that have special features like cloth covers and Velcro

to latch on to your cart. Assign each pocket a category, and store your clipped coupons or folded-up inserts inside.

✦ **PROS.** A coupon wallet is definitely the most stylish option. While binder-wielding couponers can sometimes be considered a bit on the fanatical side, women with chic coupon clutches are more likely to get, "Dang, I wish I was like her!" comments. More important than that, of course, is that fact that they're versatile and easy to take with you.

✦ **CONS.** Unlike with a coupon binder, you'll have to take the coupons out of each pocket to see them all, and you'll probably find yourself coming up with secondary organizational systems like envelopes or paperclips. And if you have a giant coupon collection, you could very well outgrow the wallet.

EXTREME TIP

In addition keeping a space in your coupon wallet for coupons you plan on using on this week's shopping trip, you may also want to keep a space open. That way, while you're on your trip, you can move the coupons from one section to the other when you put the item you're looking for into your cart.

COUPON BOX

If your mother had a coupon collection, it was probably in a box. This method is basically an expanded envelope system—place index cards with categories written on them standing up in your box, and use envelopes to store the coupons in that category. (This will work best if you use a box that matches the size of your envelopes. The smaller size letter envelopes usually work best.) You may also want to cut the flaps off the envelopes to make your coupons easier to get at. When it's time to go shopping, take only the coupons you need with you, or bring the entire box along.

✦ **PROS.** The sky is the limit when it comes to using a box system. Envelopes and index cards are much cheaper (and easier to come by) than plastic holders for coupons inside binders, so you'll feel more comfortable experimenting with different ways to organize your coupon stash. Many people also prefer flipping through their organized box to flipping through pages of a binder.

✦ **CONS.** Unlike a coupon binder, it's harder to quickly see each and every one of your coupons. If you do decide to take your box to the store, it can be a bit

unwieldy...most will fit in the front seat of your cart, but many of us will have a kid in there! You may have the best luck with a plastic storage container with a snap-on lid.

NO-CLIP METHOD

Our favorite method for organizing coupons, the no-clip method works by organizing your coupon inserts rather than the coupons themselves. Use your existing filing cabinet or an expanding file to simply save all the coupon inserts from your Sunday paper by date. Then, when you're checking out coupon matchups online (visit WhoKnewTips.com/ExtremeCoupons for our favorite sites), simply go find the insert that has the coupon you need. Cut it out and put it in your shopping-trip envelope or coupon wallet.

✦ **PROS.** Because you don't have to clip individual coupons—or even look inside the inserts—this method is definitely the fastest. If you find yourself printing coupons off the internet before you see them linked up on coupon matchup sites, create a separate folder for internet-printed coupons, and sort them by source if you have a lot.

✦ CONS. If you don't usually match up your coupons with sales using matchup sites, this method probably won't work well for you. It's much harder to know what coupons you have at any given moment, and you'll probably end up hanging onto a lot of expired coupons. It's also a bit of a pain to take to the store with you, and since it's not organized by product it can take a long time to find a matching coupon for an unadvertised sale.

WHO KNEW?

Not sure which date your coupon insert came from? Take a look near the fold. Just about every insert will have the date printed on the front, sideways, close to the "spine."

Organizing Your Stockpile

As you've probably realized, the key to making extreme couponing work is to stock up on items when they're at rock-bottom prices, so you don't have to buy them until they're on sale again. Of course, you're going to need somewhere to put all this stuff! As with organizing your coupons, use whatever system works best for you. But your stockpiling needs will increase as your extreme couponing skills do! Here is what you need to consider when stockpiling.

SECRETS TO STOCKPILING

You may want to start with emptying out a kitchen cabinet for your stockpile, but if your kitchen is anything like ours, you probably don't have an easily accessible cabinet that you can empty out (without having to find someplace else to keep your blender attachments and punch bowl). Instead, we suggest setting up some inexpensive shelving somewhere in your home where you have a little space—a basement, laundry room, even a guest room! Another option is purchasing a plastic chest of drawers or sealable containers. It may seem like a pain to have to set aside part of your home, but don't forget that going to your basement is much easier than running to the store!

When you're just beginning to build a stockpile, a cabinet or plastic storage container or two may be enough. Later on, you will probably want to move to a bigger space. No matter where your stockpile is, there are a few things to keep in mind in terms of its organization:

✦ **SEEING YOUR STOCKPILE.** You might not think it's possible to forget that you have 20 packages of Rice-A-Roni in your basement, but as your stockpile grows,

it will be harder and harder to keep track of what you have! So make sure you know what's in your stockpile—that way you'll ensure you don't accidentally buy more of it at the store. If you don't have room to keep everything in plain sight, keep a list of every product you own, along with their quantities.

✦ **EXPIRATION DATES.** Of course, if items you've purchased expire before you use them, then all your hard work has gone to waste! So it's important to keep track of each product's shelf life. Write the expiration date on a Post-It note and place it near the products. Or, if you're keeping track of your stockpile on a list, mark the expiration dates next to each item on the list.

✦ **WHAT GOES WHERE.** Along with this, many people use a "first in, first out" system for their stockpile, similar to what stores use. This means that when they get new products, they put them behind the old products, ensuring that the oldest products get used first. It's also important to take some time to figure out how your stockpile should be arranged. We keep items that we use less frequently, like cleaning supplies, on higher shelves, and items we may use for dinner at eye level. Do whatever works best for you—it's your store!

WHAT TO STOCKPILE

An easy answer to the question, "What should I stockpile?" is "Everything that you'll use before it goes bad!" But some things are easier to stockpile than others. When you're first beginning to stockpile, an easy place to start is with paper and home goods like garbage bags, aluminum foil, and cleaning supplies. Since they never go bad, you won't have to worry about buying too many or making sure your stockpile is super organized.

A better question might be, "What shouldn't I stockpile?" Believe it or not, it's easy to get out of hand with the stockpiling. If you're running out of space or have more items than you feel your family could use in a year, you may be going too far. We also recommend trying products before you stockpile them (even if you can get a great price). Kids can be finicky, and even though they love one brand of apple juice, they might outright reject another brand, even if you only bought it for mere cents a bottle. Of course, you can always donate products you don't use, but no one wants to be stuck trying to get rid of 15 jugs of apple juice (trust us on this one—they won't fit in your purse).

WHO KNEW?

It might be tempting, but we don't recommend storing items in your garage. Since it isn't climate controlled, it's easy to ruin even non-food items like lotion and makeup. Secondly, there are so many chemicals in your garage that it's hard to keep fumes from permeating your stockpile. If you're really running out of room, though, there are a few items you can keep there. Razors, soap and shampoo, laundry and cleaning supplies, baby wipes, toilet paper, Band-Aids, and air fresheners are a few.

STOCKING YOUR FREEZER

Nothing gives us more pride than looking in our freezer and seeing all the bargains we've bought that are ready to be consumed! Many couponers buy an additional freezer for all their finds—check eBay and Craigslist for inexpensive second-hand freezers. Some people prefer upright freezers because it's easier to see everything inside, while others prefer chest freezers for their ample space and energy-saving design (it's much harder for that expensive cold air to spill out of a chest freezer). No matter which kind you choose, again, make sure you stay organized with either a list of what's inside or the ability to see what you have. You may want to use plastic bins or milk cartons to further subdivide the space in your chest freezer.

Don't forget that you can freeze much more than meat and TV dinners! Some surprising items you may not realize you can freeze are:

✦ **MILK.** Freeze milk right in its carton, or separate into several containers and freeze those. If you use skim milk, it can be thawed and drank later and you'll never be able to tell the difference in taste. For other varieties of milk, shake after thawing, then use in sauces and baking.

✦ **CHEESE.** Believe it or not, you can successfully freeze many varieties of cheese without them loosing their taste or texture. Cut into small blocks, place in sealed plastic bags, and then keep in the freezer for when you need them. Cheese varieties that can be successfully frozen are Brick, Cheddar, Edam, Gouda, Muenster, Port du Salut, Swiss, Provolone, Mozzarella, and Camembert. Small cheeses, such as Camembert, can even be frozen in their original packages. When removed from the freezer, cheese should be put in the refrigerator and used as soon as possible after thawing.

✦ **FRUIT.** If you're not going to eat it raw, you can freeze fruit and use later in baked goods, smoothies, or other applications. Berries are especially easy to freeze—place them in a single layer on a cookie sheet and place

the sheet in the freezer. Once they're frozen, you can transfer them to a resealable plastic bag and save. If you enjoy lemon in your drinking water, cut your lemons in slices, then freeze between pieces of wax paper for later. And if you want to save ripe tomatoes for your famous spaghetti sauce, here's a neat trick: Core them and freeze them in an airtight container. When you're ready to use them in sauces, soups, or stews, hold each frozen tomato under warm running water and the skin will peel right off.

✦ **VEGETABLES.** Again, as long as you're not eating them raw, you can freeze most vegetables. We recommend chopping them first, then freezing them in resealable plastic bags. Once the bags have frozen, you can set them upright, saving you lots of room in your freezer.

✦ **BREAD.** Many people don't realize that you can freeze sliced bread. If you're making toast you can stick a frozen slice right in the toaster frozen, or leave a few slices covered on the counter for about 10 minutes to thaw. The best part is that if you're making sandwiches for your kids' lunches, you don't even need to wait—it will thaw by lunchtime, and peanut butter is much easier to spread on the frozen bead.

Couponing Glossary

Extreme couponers have their very own lingo, so in case you see anything on a website (or in this book) you don't understand, here's a cheat sheet for you. Any further questions? Contact us anytime at WhoKnewTips.com!

$1/1 OR OTHER RATIOS - Ratios are often used to quickly state what kind of coupon it is. $1/1 means a coupon for $1 off one item. $2.50/4 would mean a coupon for $2.50 off when you buy four items. Etc.

AY - A coupon found in All You magazine

AC - After coupon

AR - After rebate

BLINKIES - Coupons that are obtained from an in-aisle coupon dispenser at the grocery store (usually found with blinking lights on top)

BOGO (OR B1G1) - A buy one, get one free coupon or offer

BTFE - Box Tops for Education, a program that allows you to save box tops to donate money to schools. Some couponers will trade for these proofs of purchase. BTFE also offers coupons on their website.

BTGO (OR B2G1) - A buy two, get one free coupon or offer

CATALINA COUPON (CAT) - Coupons that print up at the register from a box called a Catalina machine. These coupons are rewarded based on the purchases you make.

COUPON CLIPPING SERVICES (CCS) - Companies that cut coupons for you, and allow you to pay on a per-coupon basis for them. For a list of Coupon clipping services, visit WhoKnewTips.com/ExtremeCoupons.

COUPON INFORMATION CORPORATION (CIC) - A not-for-profit association dedicated to fighting coupon fraud and promoting ethical couponing, comprised of most coupon-issuers in the United States

CRT - A coupon that prints along with your receipt (or Cash Register Tape). At CVS, CRTs can also be coupons that you obtain from their coupon machine

DND - Do not double – If your supermarket would ordinarily double this coupon, this particular coupon will not be doubled

DNT - Do not triple – If your supermarket would ordinarily triple this coupon, this particular coupon will not be tripled

DOUBLING - When a store offers you twice the value of your coupon. For instance, if your coupon is for 25¢ off, if a store doubles, it will be worth 50¢ off

ECB - ExtraCare Bucks, coupons that give you money off at CVS

ESR - Walgreens Easy Saver, a coupon-filled promotion that is released once a month at Walgreens

ETS - Excludes trial sizes

EXP - Expiration date

IP (OR IPC) - An internet-printed coupon

IVC - A coupon from the Walgreens' monthly Instant Value Coupon Book

IR - Instant Rebate

FAR - Free after rebate

FILLER ITEM - A low-priced item like gum or a trial size that you purchase because the store you're shopping at doesn't give you cash or credit for overages

FS - Free shipping

GC - Gift card

GM - A Sunday-paper coupon insert released by General Mills. A date will usually accompany this abbreviation on coupon sites to let you know which exact insert the coupon is in.

MIR - Mail-in rebate

MANUFACTURER COUPON (MFR OR MQ) - A coupon issued by a manufacturer of a product

MATCHUP - A recent coupon that matches up with a sale or other coupon for the same product

MONEY-MAKER (MM) - A matchup that will leave you with an overage

NED - No expiration date

NLA - No longer available

OOP - Money spent out-out-pocket

OOS - Out of stock—when a store has run out of a product

OVERAGE - When a coupon or stack of coupons exceeds the sale price of an item. For instance, if an item is on sale for 75¢ and you have a coupon for $1 off, your overage is 25¢

OYNO - On your next order

P&G - A Sunday-paper coupon insert released by Proctor & Gamble. A date will usually accompany this abbreviation on coupon sites to let you know which exact insert the coupon is in.

PEELIES - Coupons that are peeled from the side of a product

PSA - Prices starting at

Q - Coupon

REGIONAL (R) - A deal that varies by region

RP - A Sunday-paper coupon insert released by Red Plum. A date will usually accompany this abbreviation on coupon sites to let you know which exact insert the coupon is in.

RR - Register Rewards, cash-back coupons from Walgreens

SCR - Single Check Rebates, a Rite Aid rewards program

SS - A Sunday-paper coupon insert released by SmartSource. A date will usually accompany this abbreviation on coupon sites to let you know which exact insert the coupon is in.

STACKING - Using more than one coupon for the same item

STOCKPILE - As a noun, a stash of food and home items you have on-hand. As a verb, the act of buying all of these items while they're on sale.

STORE COUPON - A coupon issued by a store that can only be used at that particular store. Usually found in store circulars or on their website.

TEAR PADS - Pads of coupons that are sometimes attached to the shelves at supermarkets.

TRANSACTION - A purchase at the cash register. If you pay and receive a receipt, that is considered a transaction. With couponing, it can sometimes benefit you to make more than one transaction, if the cashier will allow it.

UPC - The barcode that appears on products that is scanned when it's being rung up

UPR - +UP Rewards, a rewards program at Rite Aid

VV - Video Values coupons, which you can obtain by watching commercials on Rite Aid's website

WINETAG (WT) - A coupon found on a wine bottle

WSL - While supplies last

WYB - When you buy

V - A Valassis Sunday paper coupon insert, also known as the Red Plum or RP insert

YMMV - Your mileage may vary, meaning that the deal may be different in different regions

who knew?
online

Visit us on the web at WhoKnewTips.com!

* Money-saving tips
* Quick 'n' easy recipes
* Who Knew? products
* And much more!

Twitter.com/WhoKnewTips
Get a free daily tip and ask us your questions

YouTube.com/WhoKnewTips
Watch demos of your favorite tips

Facebook.com/WhoKnewTips
Daily tips, giveaways, and more fun!